BESIDE THE SEASIDE

BESIDE THE SEASIDE

CAROLYN CALDICOTT · PHOTOGRAPHS BY CHRIS CALDICOTT

Pimpernel
Press ltd
www.pimpernelpress.com

Pimpernel Press Limited
www.pimpernelpress.com

Beside the Seaside
Copyright © Pimpernel Press Limited 2015
Text copyright © Carolyn Caldicott 2015
Photographs copyright © Chris Caldicott 2015
First Pimpernel Press edition 2015
Designed by Becky Clarke

A catalogue record for this book is available
from the British Library.

ISBN 978-1-9102-5843-9

Typeset in Clarendon LT
Printed and bound in China

9 8 7 6 5 4 3 2 1

CONTENTS

INTRODUCTION

There is something terribly exciting about the prospect of a day by the seaside. The very phrase is full of evocative memories and nostalgia for the long, lazy bucket-and-spade days of the past. Spending the day crabbing and rock-pooling, while the folks settle into deckchairs behind a striped windshield. Lips blue with cold from braving the sea just a little too long, and burying each other in the sand to warm up. Sandcastles, seagulls and sunsets. And, on less clement days, wrapping up warm for bracing walks along the dazzling coastline. To make the day complete, of course, you need the perfect picnic. *Beside the Seaside* is packed full of no-nonsense recipes to get you out of the kitchen and into the sunshine without a soggy sandwich in sight. Here are delicious ideas for portable feasts and beach barbecues, ice creams and milkshakes, and the very best recipes inspired by the sea to help take the seaside home.

PICNICS &
PACKED LUNCHES

When we are blessed with perfect summer weather or a crisp winter day, it's time to head to the beach with a mouth-watering picnic, a portable feast that will withstand the elements and the bumpy ride in a backpack. For a quick getaway, here are recipes that are quick to prepare and good to share, combined with picnic favourites made on rainy days and stored in the freezer.

PICNIC ESSENTIALS

Take your pick from the perfect savoury picnic fillers
on the following pages.

AVOCADO & CRISPY BACON TORTILLA WRAPS

A great way to use up crispy bacon leftovers from breakfast butties, tortilla wraps will beat the bumpiest ride and stay perfectly formed.

MAKES 6
6 rashers streaky bacon, rind removed
2 ripe avocados
A good squeeze of lemon juice
Tabasco to taste
Salt and freshly ground black pepper
8 sweet cherry tomatoes, diced
A handful of rocket leaves
6 medium-sized tortilla wraps
Kitchen foil to wrap

Grill the bacon rashers until the fat becomes golden brown. Drain on a sheet of kitchen paper – the bacon will crisp as it cools. Chop the crispy bacon into thin slices and set aside until ready to start wrapping.

Cut the avocados in half, remove the stones and scoop the flesh into a bowl. Add a good squeeze of lemon juice, a dash of Tabasco and seasoning to taste. Mash the avocado roughly with the back of a fork, then stir in the diced tomato.

In a hot frying pan, lightly toast a tortilla until it becomes soft and pliable. Place it on a board and lay some rocket leaves in the centre of the lower half, spoon a portion of the avocado mixture on top and sprinkle with crispy bacon. Fold the nearside edge and sides of the tortilla over the filling and roll tightly.

Repeat the process with the remaining filling and tortillas. Wrap each rolled tortilla in kitchen foil to make a sturdy package.

SALMON AND DILL PUFF PASTRY PATTIES

———◆———

These patties are a breeze to make if you use ready-rolled puff pastry. For an effortless early morning getaway, bake the night before.

MAKES 4
375g/13oz ready-rolled puff pastry
275g/10oz thin skinless salmon fillets
A handful of baby spinach leaves, stalks removed
4 tablespoons thick sour cream
2 teaspoons butter
1 tablespoon roughly chopped dill
Grated zest of an unwaxed lemon
Salt and freshly ground black pepper
1 small free-range egg, beaten

Preheat the oven to 200°C/400°F/gas mark 6.

Unroll the puff pastry on to a board and cut into four equal-sized oblongs.

Divide the salmon fillets into four portions and trim to fit snugly on one half of the pastry oblong and leave enough room for a border to seal the pastry edges.

Cover the salmon with a few spinach leaves and season with salt and black pepper to taste. Spoon a tablespoon of sour cream and ½ teaspoon of butter on top, then sprinkle with the chopped dill and the lemon zest.

Brush the edges of the pastry with beaten egg and fold the pastry over the filling until the edges meet. Firmly crimp the edges together, brush the top with beaten egg and cut a small slit in the middle.

Place the patties on a non-stick baking tray and bake in the preheated oven for 25–30 minutes, or until they are golden brown and puffed up.

Allow to cool before packing in a protective picnic box.

CHEESE & WATERCRESS SCONES
FILLED WITH SMOKED TROUT & HORSERADISH CREAM

◆——◆

These moist scones freeze brilliantly. Make them in batches and store in the freezer, ready and waiting for impromptu picnics.

If horseradish cream is too strong for little mouths, you can replace with soft cream cheese. Fresh goat's cheese also makes a good option. Or, for something completely different, serve the scones ploughman style with chunks of Cheddar cheese, pickle and apple slices.

MAKES 12 SCONES

The scones
200g/7oz self–raising flour
75g/3oz wholemeal flour
1 teaspoon baking powder
75g/3oz butter, cut into small cubes
50g/2oz watercress leaves, finely chopped
75g/3oz mature Cheddar cheese, grated
1 medium free-range egg
Salt and freshly ground black pepper to taste
Full-fat milk to bind the scones and brush the tops

To fill the scones
Horseradish cream made with crème fraîche (1 heaped tablespoon per
    scone) flavoured with a squeeze of lemon juice and hot horseradish
    sauce and seasoning to taste
Sliced smoked trout
Watercress

Preheat the oven to 200°C/400°F/gas mark 6.
Sift the flour and baking powder into a bowl. Lightly rub in the butter until the mixture resembles breadcrumbs. Stir in the chopped watercress and three-quarters of the grated cheese, and add seasoning to taste.

Beat the egg with 3 tablespoons of milk and gradually combine with the mixture until a stiff dough forms (if the dough seems dry add a little more milk).

Place the dough on a floured surface, roll out until approximately 2.5cm/1inch thick and cut into 5cm/2 inch-diameter rounds. Brush the scones with milk and sprinkle with the remaining grated cheese.

Place the scones on a non-stick baking tray and bake in the preheated oven for 15–20 minutes, until they are golden brown.

Fill each scone with a dollop of the horseradish cream, a coil of smoked trout and a sprig of watercress.

GOURMET SAUSAGE ROLLS

Homemade sausage rolls beat ready-made hands down. The great thing is being able to choose the type and quality of meat filling. Stick to conventional pork sausage meat or remove the skins from good-quality sausages.

Sausage rolls can be frozen before baking. If cooking from frozen, add an extra 10 minutes to the cooking time.

MAKES 20 MINI ROLLS
1 small onion, finely chopped
75g/3oz button brown cap mushrooms, finely chopped
A splash of sunflower oil
50g/12oz sausage meat or sausages with their skins removed
   (or finely chopped vegetarian sausages)
1 dessertspoon chopped sage
1 teaspoon chopped thyme
A good grate of nutmeg
375g/13oz ready-rolled puff pastry
1 small free-range egg, beaten
Salt and freshly ground black pepper

Preheat the oven to 200°C/400°F/gas mark 6.

Fry the chopped onion and mushrooms in a splash of sunflower oil until soft but not brown. Allow the mixture to cool a little before combining with the sausage meat, herbs, nutmeg and seasoning to taste.

Unroll the puff pastry on to a board and cut lengthways down the middle into two equal-sized long strips.

Divide the filling in half. Place one half down the centre of each pastry strip and mould into a rough sausage shape. Brush the pastry edges with beaten egg and fold the pastry over the top of the filling to make a tight roll. Press along the edges to ensure a good seal.

Carefully turn the rolls over, brush the tops with beaten egg and cut each one into approximately ten equal portions (you can make them larger if you prefer).

Place the sausage rolls on a non-stick baking tray and cook in the oven for 25–30 minutes, until puffed up and golden.

CRISPY PROSCIUTTO & ASPARAGUS FRITTATAS

Individual frittatas baked in a muffin tin are perfect for a picnic. Replace sliced asparagus tips with diced baby courgettes or podded fresh peas as a seasonal variation.

MAKES 8
Olive oil
8 slices prosciutto, cut in half across the middle
2 tablespoons olive oil, plus extra to grease the muffin tin
4 large free-range eggs
55ml/2 fl oz single cream
75g/3oz asparagus tips, sliced
   (or diced baby courgettes or podded fresh peas)
6 spring onions, thinly sliced
8 basil leaves, finely chopped
50g/2oz grated Parmesan cheese
 Salt and freshly ground black pepper

Preheat the oven to 190°C/375°F/Gas mark 5.

Grease eight indents of a muffin tin with olive oil and line with the prosciutto, taking care not to leave any gaps.

Whisk the eggs and cream together until light and fluffy. Add the asparagus, the spring onions, the chopped basil leaves and three-quarters of the grated Parmesan cheese. Season to taste and stir together until well combined.

Divide the mixture between the prosciutto-lined muffin tin indents and sprinkle the remaining cheese on top. Carefully transfer to the preheated oven and bake for 25–30 minutes, until the prosciutto is crisp and the filling just set.

Allow the frittatas to cool before removing from the tin (a small blunt knife comes in handy at this stage).

PITTA POCKETS

Avoid soggy sandwiches with these superbly robust pitta pockets. Stock your store cupboard with jars of roasted peppers, pesto, tapenade and tahini – handy ready-made ingredients that instantly transform pitta pockets into something rather wonderful. Feta and halloumi cheese also have a relatively long shelf life and are well worth having in the fridge.

Lightly toast each pitta bread until soft and puffed up, cut in half widthwise, prise open and get stuffing!

FABULOUS PITTA FILLINGS

GREEK SALAD DRIZZLED WITH A TAPENADE DRESSING

Combine equal quantities of chopped cucumber and tomato with a little sliced Cos lettuce and a scattering of mint leaves. Add a generous quantity of crumbled feta cheese and finely sliced red onion to taste. Pack the salad inside warm pitta pockets and dress with equal quantities of tapenade and olive oil whisked with a squeeze of lemon juice (allow approximately one tablespoon of dressing per pitta).

GRIDDLED HALLOUMI AND COURGETTES WITH LEMONY TAHINI DRESSING

Slice equal quantities of halloumi cheese and courgette (cut lengthways), brush with olive oil and cook on a hot griddle (or under a grill) until chargrilled and soft. Pop inside toasted pitta along with slices of juicy plum tomato and crispy watercress. Whisk together equal quantities of tahini, natural yoghurt and olive oil, add a good squeeze of lemon juice to thin the dressing and season to taste. Drizzle a tablespoon or so inside each pitta.

HUMMUS

Hummus makes a fantastic filler. Spruce it up with a scoop of ready-made pesto: – you can try rocket, red pepper or sun-dried tomato or stick to more traditional basil. Add as little or as much pesto as you like and fill each pitta along with slices of roast red pepper (available in jars) and rocket leaves.

PESTO

Pesto is also rather good mixed with a dollop of mayonnaise and thick Greek yoghurt, combine with shredded cooked chicken breast, a little grated lemon zest and seasoning to taste. Pile the chicken mixture inside the pitta and top with a small handful of crisp pea shoots.

Whichever filling you choose, wrap the completed pittas in greaseproof paper.

SEASIDE SAVOURY DIPS

Add to your five-a-day with seaside savoury dips and crunchy vegetable crudités.

Each recipe makes a medium-sized bowl for sharing. Scoop into a tub with a fitted lid and store in the fridge until ready to pack your picnic. Prepare a selection of crudités and pop into a plastic bag.

PEA, MINT & PUMPKIN SEED DIP

Frozen peas are transformed in minutes into a dip full of fresh flavours. Fresh or frozen broad beans are also very tasty in this recipe.

250g/9oz frozen peas
A small bunch of mint leaves, roughly chopped
1 garlic clove, crushed
2 tablespoons pumpkin seed butter (cashew nut butter is also good)
Juice of ½ a lemon
2 tablespoons olive oil
Salt and freshly ground black pepper

Defrost the frozen peas for a couple of minutes in boiling water. Drain and refresh in cold water until cool.

Blend the peas in a food processor with the mint, garlic and pumpkin seed butter until roughly chopped.

Add the lemon juice, olive oil and seasoning to taste and blend until smooth but still retaining a few lumpy bits.

BEANIE DIP WITH ZA'TAR SPICE MIX

You can use almost any tin of beans from the store cupboard in this recipe: butter beans, cannellini, flageolet, ful, black beans . . . To make a more conventional hummus-style dip use chickpeas and pass on the cumin seeds.

Za'tar spice is readily available to buy, but it is also rather satisfying to make your own. Mix two tablespoons of toasted sesame seeds, dried thyme and oregano with two teaspoons of ground cumin and sumac (or paprika) and store in a sealed jar until needed.

400g/14oz tin cannellini beans, drained
1 garlic clove, crushed
1 teaspoon cumin seeds
Juice of ½ a lemon
2 tablespoons olive oil
2 tablespoons tahini
Salt and freshly ground black pepper
1 heaped tablespoon toasted pine nuts to garnish
Za'tar spice to taste

Drain the beans (reserving two tablespoons of the liquid for later), and blend in a food processor with the garlic, cumin and lemon juice until finely chopped. Add the retained liquid, olive oil, tahini and seasoning to taste and whizz together until smooth.

Scoop the dip into a tub and sprinkle with pine nuts and za'tar spice mix.

COOLERS FOR LAZY SUMMER DAYS

Icy-cold chillers to keep you cool, calm and collected.

WATERMELON GAZPACHO

Watermelon gazpacho is a great cooler on heady hot summer days. If you have a supply of gazpacho in the freezer, pour the just-defrosted soup into a thermos flask and it will stay perfectly chilled until lunchtime.

MAKES 4–6 PORTIONS
560g/1lb 4oz ripe plum tomatoes, cubed
450g/1lb deseeded, cubed watermelon
1 small red pepper, deseeded and roughly chopped
5 spring onions, sliced
1 garlic clove, crushed
1 red chilli, sliced (optional)
4 tablespoons olive oil
2 tablespoons sherry or red wine vinegar
A good squeeze of lemon juice
Salt and freshly ground black pepper to taste

Blend the tomatoes in a food processor until smooth, pass through a sieve to remove the pips and return to the food processor.

Add the remaining ingredients and pulse together until the soup is smooth but still retains some texture. Finally adjust the vinegar and seasoning to taste before chilling in the fridge.

PINK LEMONADE

No picnic is complete without lashings of homemade lemonade, and pink lemonade is pretty as a picture. Pour over a handful of ice cubes in a thermos flask or alternatively freeze the lemonade in plastic bottles (filled three-quarters full). The frozen lemonade will gradually defrost, keeping everything cool.

MAKES ABOUT 1.2 LITRES/2 PINTS
The grated zest and juice of 6 large unwaxed lemons
1 small punnet raspberries, crushed through a sieve
150g/5oz caster sugar
1 litre/1¾ pints boiling water
Extra slices of lemon to serve

Place the lemon zest and juice in a large bowl, add the crushed raspberries and caster sugar and stir in the boiling water until the sugar has completely dissolved.

Leave the mixture to cool, then cover and place in the fridge overnight.

Sieve to remove the grated zest, pour into bottles and chill in the fridge. Serve over ice with extra slices of lemon.

WARMERS TO FILL THE THERMOS FLASK

Warm the cockles of your heart with a cup of hot soup
or aromatic chai tea.

CREAMY CARROT & LENTIL SOUP

Pop a thermos flask of this nourishing soup into your backpack with a piece of fruit for a portable lunch to keep you going all day. To ensure the soup stays piping hot, warm the thermos flask first with boiling water.

MAKES 4–6 PORTIONS
275g/10oz split red lentils
1 large onion, diced
2 cloves garlic, finely chopped
3 tablespoons butter
1 teaspoon ground cumin
½ teaspoon smoked paprika
275g/10oz grated carrot
1½ litre/2½ pints vegetable stock
120ml/4floz single cream
Salt and freshly ground black pepper

Rinse the red lentils in cold water until the water runs clear.

Fry the onion and garlic in the butter until soft but not brown. Add the cumin and paprika, fry for one minute, then stir in the grated carrot. Cover the pan and sweat the vegetables for a couple of minutes before adding the washed lentils.

Pour in the stock, stir well and gently simmer (stirring at regular intervals) until the lentils are soft and starting to break down.

Whizz the soup with a hand blender until smooth then stir in the cream and seasoning to taste. If the soup is too thick, add extra water.

SPICED CHAI TEA

Pause for a while with a cup of hot spiced chai tea and your favourite view.

MAKES 570ml/1 PINT
275ml/½ pint full-fat milk
275ml/½ pint water
½ teaspoon ground ginger or
   1 tablespoon finely chopped fresh root ginger
½ teaspoon ground cinnamon
⅓ teaspoon ground black pepper
⅓ teaspoon ground cardamom
3 cloves
A good grate of nutmeg
3 Assam tea bags
Brown sugar or honey to taste

Pour the milk and water into a milk pan, whisk in the spices and heat together until bubbles start to form around the edge of the pan.

Add the tea bags and gently simmer, stirring regularly, for a further 5 minutes.

Discard the tea bags, add sugar to taste and strain the tea into a warmed thermos flask.

SUGAR RUSH

Sweet treats to fuel beach games and cliff walks.

HONEY GRANOLA BARS

Oatie bars packed full of slow-energy-release nuts, seeds and dried fruit.

MAKES 12 BARS
75g/3oz butter
120ml/4 fl oz runny honey
2 tablespoons soft brown sugar
1 teaspoon ground cinnamon
Pinch of sea salt
150g/5oz rolled oats
110g/4oz chopped almonds
50g/2oz sunflower seeds
20g/¾oz linseeds
110g/4oz mix of chopped dried apricots, prunes and dates

Preheat the oven to 180°C/350°F/gas mark 6 and line a 20-cm/8-inch square baking tray with baking parchment.

Warm the butter, honey and sugar over a low heat until the butter and sugar melt, whisk in the cinnamon and salt.

Combine the remaining ingredients in a bowl and stir in the butter mixture. Gently knead together for a couple of minutes until clumps start to form.

Pile into the lined tin and press the mixture firmly with the back of a spoon until compacted.

Place the tin in the preheated oven and bake for 30 minutes until golden brown. Leave the granola to set and cool in the tin before cutting into 12 bars.

BLACKBERRY & APPLE MUFFINS

Moist muffins always travel well, especially if you line the muffin tin with a square of baking parchment cut large enough to protect the tops.

This recipe is very versatile. You can use the basic batter mixture to create all manner of muffins, simply substituting an equal quantity of fruit and spices of your choice for the blackberries and apples. Grated vegetables also work well.

Looking for inspiration? Fail-safe flavour combinations include mashed banana and cardamom; blueberries and vanilla extract; chopped pear and ground ginger; grated carrot, orange zest and allspice; grated beetroot and chocolate chips.

MAKES 8
200g/7oz plain flour
1 dessertspoon baking powder
Good pinch of salt
50g/2oz butter
75g/3oz soft brown sugar,
    plus extra to sprinkle on top
1 tablespoon maple syrup
1 scant teaspoon ground cinnamon
1 large free-range egg
110ml/4 fl oz full-fat milk
1 sweet apple, cored, peeled and grated
110g/4oz blackberries
Small handful oats
Small handful sunflower seeds

Preheat the oven to 180°C/375°F/gas mark 5.

Line a muffin tin with 8 squares of greaseproof paper (cut large enough to poke over the top of each indent).

Sift the flour, baking powder and salt into a bowl.

Melt the butter over a low heat and stir in the sugar, maple syrup and cinnamon. Allow the mixture to cool a little while you prepare the egg mixture (the egg will scramble if the mixture is too hot).

Beat the egg and milk together until light and fluffy. Gradually whisk in the cooled spiced butter and when well combined fold into the sifted flour. Add the grated apple and two-thirds of the blackberries.

Divide the batter between the indents of the muffin tin. Stud the top of each muffin with the remaining blackberries and sprinkle with oats, sunflower seeds and a little extra sugar to taste. Bake in the preheated oven for 35–40 minutes until golden (the tops should spring back when gently pressed).

CHOCOLATE, CRANBERRY & MARSHMALLOW TRAY BAKE

This chunky chocolate tray bake spiked with marshmallows and cranberries is rich enough to serve without a sticky topping.

MAKES 12 SQUARES
225g/8oz self-raising flour
4 tablespoons cocoa
1 teaspoon baking powder
250g/9oz soft butter
250g/9oz golden caster sugar
1 teaspoon vanilla extract
4 medium free-range eggs
16 marshmallows cut into quarters
200g/7oz fresh or frozen cranberries, cut in half

Preheat the oven to 180°C/350°F/gas mark 4 and line an oblong cake tin (approximately 30cm/12 inches x 20cm/8 inches) with baking parchment.

Sieve the flour, cocoa and baking powder into a bowl.

Cream the butter, sugar and vanilla extract together until light and fluffy. Whisk in each egg separately and fold in the sieved flour mixture. Gently stir in the marshmallows and cranberries.

Scoop the mixture into the prepared tin, level the top and bake in the preheated oven for 35–40 minutes, until a skewer inserted in the middle comes out clean.

When the tin is cool enough to handle, turn the tray bake out and carefully peel away the baking parchment. Place on a wire rack and when completely cool cut into 12 equal-sized pieces.

BEACHSIDE BARBECUES

There is nothing quite like the flavour of sizzling-hot chargrilled fish straight from the barbecue, with the tempting aroma of succulent smoky flesh and crispy blistered skin. All you need is the freshest possible fish, tasty marinades, tongue-tingling sauces, veggies and maybe a salad or two. Add a bunch of friends and family, cold beer, the sand between your toes and you can't go wrong.

To satisfy anyone with a sweet tooth, pack some ripe soft fruit and marshmallows to caramelize over the dying embers of the barbecue. As the sun sinks into the sea, toast the glorious day with a rip-roaring chorus of favourite campfire tunes.

RAINY DAYS

On rainy days recreate the recipes back home using a smoking hot griddle
pan or a preheated grill.

TOP TIPS TO GET YOU STARTED

The barbecue needs to burn for at least 15 minutes before the serious business of cooking can begin. If the coals are too hot you run the risk of thicker barbecue ingredients becoming burnt on the outside while they are still uncooked on the inside. The coals are ready when the smoke stops and the embers glow. Work out your barbecue pecking order, placing ingredients that require quick cooking over a high heat, such as shellfish, squid and sardines, on the grill at the beginning of the barbecue, when the coals are at their hottest, and leaving thicker ingredients that need a slower approach until the temperature of the coals has started to drop.

Allow all ingredients to warm to room temperature before placing on the grill. To prevent bamboo skewers burning, soak in water for 30 minutes or so before threading with ingredients,

Chunky fish, meat and vegetables can be marinated overnight, but salt and citrus juices should be added no more than two hours before cooking. Thin fillets and small fish only need to marinate for a short time – the time it takes for the barbie to die down once lit is plenty. Prepare marinades the night before, pop into a container with a tight-fitting lid and store in the fridge.

Take care to oil your barbecue ingredients only lightly – any excess oil will drip on to the coals and create a fog of smoke. Stick to sunflower oil or light olive oil (a barbecue is too hot for extra virgin).

It's worth investing in a mesh barbecue cage to cook smaller fish, which have an annoying tendency to slip between the gaps in the grill. With a cage, turning the fish becomes a breeze.

Whole fish are much more forgiving on the barbecue than fillets, which tend to break up and dry out. For the best results, stick to small or medium-sized whole fish. Oily fish such as mackerel and sardines are always a good choice: the flesh stays moist and the skin crunchy.

To test that a fish is cooked through, insert a knife into the thickest part and gently lift. The flesh should flake easily.

GRILLED SARDINES WITH HERBY CAPER SALSA VERDE

A wire-mesh cage really comes in handy when barbecuing sardines. To cook the sardines' oily flesh to chargrilled heaven, place the filled cage over the hot coals at the beginning of the barbecue.

SERVES 4
12 sardines, gutted
6 bay leaves, torn in half
1 tablespoon sunflower oil
Salt and freshly ground black pepper

The salsa verde
5 tablespoons extra virgin olive oil
Juice and zest of a lime
2 heaped tablespoons salted capers, rinsed
1 garlic clove, crushed
A small bunch of flat leaf parsley, roughly chopped
Freshly ground black pepper to taste

Whizz the salsa ingredients in a food processor until finely chopped – there is no need to add salt, the capers are salty enough. Scoop into an airtight container and place in the fridge. The salsa keeps well for a couple of days.

Rinse the sardines in water and pat dry with kitchen paper. Tuck half a bay leaf inside the cavity of each sardine and rub the skin with sunflower oil.

Generously season the fish on both sides with salt and black pepper to taste and place the sardines head to tail inside a mesh barbecue cage.

Place over the hot coals at the beginning of the barbecue and cook for 2–3 minutes on each side (depending on size) until the skin is nicely blackened and the flesh cooked through.

To serve top each fish with a spoonful of herby salsa.

CHARGRILLED MACKEREL WITH GINGER, HONEY & SOY

An excellent way to utilize a bucket full of super-fresh gleaming mackerel, the bounty of a successful fishing trip around the bay. Brush the Asian-inspired marinade over the prepared fish and leave the flavours to combine while the barbecue is reaching the correct temperature.

SERVES 4
4 mackerel, gutted and rinsed

The marinade
4 tablespoons light soy sauce
Juice and grated zest of a lime
2 tablespoons sunflower oil
1 tablespoon runny honey
1 dessertspoon sesame oil
5-cm/2-inch piece of ginger root, peeled and grated

Whisk the marinade ingredients together until well combined.

Slash the mackerel at regular intervals on each side and brush the marinade over the skin and into the flesh. Leave the mackerel to marinate until the searing heat of the barbecue has died down.

Lay the fish on the grill and cook for 4–5 minutes on each side, until the flesh is cooked through and the skin is chargrilled.

CORIANDER, CHILLI & LIME MONKFISH SKEWERS

Meaty monkfish is robust enough to thread on skewers without running the risk of losing half the fish in the fire.

If you are using bamboo skewers, remember to soak them in water for half an hour before threading.

No time to mix a marinade? Reduce the monkfish quantity by a third, top up with thick slices of chorizo, brush with oil and chargrill.

SERVES 4
800g/1lb 9oz monkfish, cut into 3cm/1¼ inch cubes

The marinade
2 plump garlic cloves, crushed
2 red chillies, seeds removed and sliced
A handful of coriander leaves
3 tablespoons olive oil
3 tablespoons natural yoghurt
Zest and juice of a lime
Salt and freshly ground black pepper to taste

Blend the marinade ingredients in a food processor until the herbs are finely chopped and the sauce is smooth.

Coat the monkfish cubes with the marinade and set aside until the barbecue coals are ready.

Thread the monkfish on soaked skewers and cook for 2 minutes on each side, until golden brown and just cooked through.

WHOLE RED MULLET STUFFED WITH CARAMELIZED ONION, FENNEL & FENUGREEK

To ensure the mullet cooks through properly without becoming burnt on the outside, cook the stuffed fish on the barbecue when the coals are glowing rather than searing hot.

Red mullet are quite scaly – ask the fishmonger to scale the fish when gutting. If red mullet is unavailable, sea bass makes a fabulous alternative.

SERVES 4
4 medium-sized red mullet, scaled, gutted and rinsed
Olive oil
1 fennel bulb, trimmed, cored and thinly sliced
1 medium red onion, thinly sliced
1 orange, sliced
2 garlic cloves, finely chopped
1 scant teaspoon ground fenugreek
Salt and freshly ground black pepper

Brush the skin and cavity of the red mullet with a little olive oil. Stuff each fish with a layer of fennel, red onion and orange and top with a sprinkling of garlic and ground fenugreek. Season the stuffing and skin with salt and black pepper to taste and place on the barbecue. Cook for 5–6 minutes on each side, until the stuffing is soft and the fish is charred on the outside and cooked through.

PIRI-PIRI JUMBO PRAWNS

Perk up jumbo prawns with an aromatic piri-piri marinade. Choose raw prawns in the shell whenever possible – the shell protects the prawns from drying out.

MAKES 16
4 tablespoons piri-piri sauce
    (see page 60)
1 tablespoons olive oil
Juice of ½ a lime
16 jumbo prawns, raw and shell on

Combine the piri-piri sauce with the olive oil and lime juice.

Coat the prawns with the piri-piri marinade and set to one side for 30 minutes or so (if you are using bamboo skewers, soak the skewers in water while the prawns are marinating).

Thread the prawns on skewers (or place in a wire fish cage) and cook for a couple of minutes on each side until they begin to turn golden brown.

BLACKENED SQUID

Add some Cajun spice to the barbecue! Spice-coated squid can be barbecued whole or cut into strips and threaded on skewers. The vegetarians among you can try coating halloumi, paneer cheese or tofu using the same method.

SERVES 4
4 squid tubes
Olive oil
Salt to taste

The spice mix
1 heaped teaspoon ground cumin
1 heaped teaspoon cracked peppercorns
1 heaped teaspoon paprika
1 heaped teaspoon dried thyme
1 heaped teaspoon dried oregano
¼ teaspoon ground cloves

To serve
Piri-piri sauce (see page 60)

Combine the spice mix and store in an airtight jar until ready to use.

Rinse the squid tubes in water and pat dry with kitchen paper.

Cut the tubes down one side with a pair of kitchen scissors, open out and lay inside-down on a board. Score a criss-cross pattern in the flesh. Brush with olive oil, season to taste with salt and coat with the spice mix. Either leave whole or cut into thick strips and thread on skewers.

Place over the hot coals at the beginning of the barbecue and cook for 1–2 minutes on each side.

Serve with piri-piri sauce.

BARBECUED SHELLS

Barbecuing shellfish couldn't be simpler – their shells double as tiny cooking pots that hold in all the juices. Oysters steam in the closed shell and conveniently pop open just when they are ready to eat, and razor clams are equally obliging. Scallops, however, must be removed from the shell and cleaned, then returned to the shell to cook. All shellfish are at their best when lightly cooked – a few minutes is plenty.

BARBECUED OYSTERS

A squeeze of lemon or a shake of hot sauce is quite enough dressing for these wonderful mouthfuls of the sea.

Scrub the oysters in cold water, discarding any shells that are damaged or remain open. Place the closed shells cup-side down over the hot coals at the start of the barbecue (the oysters will only open if the temperature is high). Remove the shells from the barbecue the moment they open, lever the shell fully open with an oyster knife (or another stout knife) and sever the muscle joining the oyster to the shell. Add a squeeze of lemon or a dash of piri-piri sauce (see page 60) and enjoy immediately. Discard any shells that fail to open.

BARBECUED RAZOR CLAMS

One of the simplest ways to cook razor clams is on a barbecue. Place the washed razor clams on the grill at the beginning of the barbecue when the coals are at their hottest and remove from the heat the moment they are fully open. Add a knob of garlic butter and allow to melt into the juices before eating straight from the shell.

Back home, razor clams can be cooked on a hot griddle pan. Flip the clams as they open and cook for a further minute before adding the garlic butter.

RAZOR CLAM FACTS

Do you remember as a child, peering into small bubbling holes that appeared in the wet sand at low tide and wondering what lurked inside? Well, it would probably have been a razor clam. Dig deep and quickly enough and the long-shelled clam will be revealed.

Razor clams are available from good fishmongers or oriental supermarkets. Their sweet flesh, which is quite a delicacy, roughly resembles a cross between squid and scallops. It's important the clams are alive when cooked. Tap the shell to test: the white sausage-shaped clam should retract – discard any that fail to do so.

When cooking, follow the shellfish rule and take care not to overcook. Once cooked, avoid the gritty stomach, and the dark foot at the end of the clam.

BARBECUED SCALLOPS

Most good fishmongers will sell scallops in their shells. Ask the fishmonger to clean the scallops, but always opt to keep the shells. The scallops should still have the orange roe attached, a real bonus for fish-lovers. Rinse the scallops and give the shells a good scrub in water. Lay a couple of scallops in the cup-shaped half-shell, add a small knob of garlic butter, a tablespoon of white wine and plenty of freshly ground black pepper. Place the filled shells on the barbecue and cook until the scallop flesh has just turned white.

GARLIC BUTTER

Everyone has a different attitude to garlic, so just customize the quantity to suit your taste. You can also vary the herbs: parsley is a classic, but sorrel, dill, coriander, tarragon, rosemary and thyme are all fine fishy companions. A pinch of spice also doesn't go amiss – try experimenting with a modest teaspoon of sweet paprika, fennel or ground cumin.

Garlic butter will keep in the fridge for up to a week and can also be frozen in portions in the freezer.

MAKES 250g/9oz
250g/9oz softened salted butter, cut into cubes
4–8 garlic cloves, crushed
The grated zest of a lemon
A handful of curly parsley, finely chopped (or herbs of your choice)
Freshly ground black pepper

Beat the softened butter with the crushed garlic until well combined, and stir in the lemon zest, chopped herbs and black pepper to taste.

NON-FISHY OPTIONS

Not a fan of fish? Pack a couple of non-fishy alternatives to satisfy all tastes.

MINI LAMB BURGERS

Lamb mince makes moist burgers. Mixed with herbs and spices and topped with smoky aubergine dip (see 'BBQ Extras', page 63) they are sublime.

MAKES 12
700g/1lb 8oz lamb mince
1 medium red onion, very finely chopped
2 garlic cloves, crushed
3 sprigs rosemary, leaves stripped and finely chopped
1 tablespoon ground coriander
1 teaspoon ground cumin
1 teaspoon paprika
A handful of chopped sun-dried tomatoes (optional)
1 medium free-range egg, beaten
Salt and freshly ground black pepper to taste
Olive oil to brush the burgers

Combine the ingredients in a bowl and (with clean hands) massage the mixture until it starts to bind together.

Divide the mixture into twelve equal portions. Roll each portion into a ball, then flatten to make a fat mini burger.

Brush the burgers with olive oil, place on the barbecue and cook to taste – I like them red in the middle, but if you prefer your burgers more well done, leave to cook for longer.

HALLOUMI AND MIXED VEG BROCHETTES

Don't forget the veggies! You can assemble these halloumi brochettes using almost any barbecue-friendly veg. For an Indian-style alternative, paneer cheese has a similar texture to halloumi with a milder creamy flavour.

MAKES ABOUT 12
275g/10oz halloumi cheese
1 red pepper
1 yellow pepper
2 medium courgettes
15 cherry tomatoes

The marinade
4 tablespoons olive oil
Juice and grated zest of half a lemon
1 tablespoon light soy sauce
1 tablespoon pomegranate molasses or honey
1 heaped teaspoon chopped thyme leaves
Freshly ground black pepper to taste

Cut the halloumi into 2-cm/¾-inch squares and cut the peppers and courgettes into similar-sized pieces. Combine the tomatoes with the prepared halloumi and vegetables in a shallow dish.

Whisk the marinade ingredients together and pour evenly over the halloumi and vegetables. Gently mix together and leave to marinate for an hour or so.

Thread a selection of the ingredients on skewers, shake away any excess marinade, and cook on the barbecue until golden brown and soft.

SALADS & SAUCES

Keep salads simple. Slaws and couscous are unbeatable: they travel well and are even more delicious when made in advance. Raise the temperature with an essential homemade hot barbecue sauce dolloped on the side.

LEMON, HERB & POMEGRANATE COUSCOUS

SERVES 4
300g/10 oz couscous or fine bulgar wheat
570ml/1 pint hot vegetable stock mixed with 1 heaped teaspoon
    harissa (or to taste)
Small bunches of parsley, coriander and mint, finely chopped
6 spring onions, thinly sliced
½ teaspoon ground cinnamon
The grated zest and juice a lemon
3 tablespoons extra virgin olive oil
A generous handful of pomegranate seeds
Freshly ground black pepper to taste

Place the couscous in a bowl, pour over the hot stock and stir briefly. When the stock is completely absorbed, fluff the couscous with a fork until all the grains are separated. Set to one side to cool.

Mix the cooled couscous with the chopped herbs, spring onions and cinnamon until well combined.

Whisk the lemon and olive oil together, season to taste, combine with the couscous and sprinkle the pomegranate seeds on top.

CELERIAC & APPLE SLAW

SERVES 4
½ medium celeriac (about 350g/12oz)
2 carrots
1 crisp apple
A small handful of raisins and walnuts, roughly chopped
3 tablespoons mayonnaise
2 tablespoons thick yoghurt
1 teaspoon Dijon mustard
Juice of ½ lemon
Salt and freshly ground black pepper

Peel the celeriac and carrots and slice into matchstick-sized pieces. Cut the apple into quarters, remove the core and cut into similar-sized pieces to the vegetables.

To make the dressing whisk the mayonnaise, yoghurt, mustard and lemon juice together and season with salt and pepper to taste.

Combine the prepared vegetables and apple, add the chopped raisins and walnuts and fold in the dressing until everything is well coated.

Pile the slaw into an airtight container and pop into the fridge to chill.

PIRI-PIRI SAUCE

You can use this versatile, lip-smacking hot sauce as a marinade or a devilish condiment. Stick to large red chillies that contribute heaps of flavour without the burn and add an extra handful of chopped coriander if you wish.

MAKES ABOUT 300ml/½ pint
8 large red chillies, stalks removed
4 garlic cloves, crushed
2 teaspoons paprika
1 teaspoon cracked black pepper
1 teaspoon fine sea salt
110ml/4 fl oz freshly squeezed lemon or lime juice
125ml/5 fl oz olive oil
A small handful of finely chopped coriander leaves (optional)

Slit the chillies down one side and scrape away the seeds. Roughly chop the chillies and blend in a food processor with the garlic, paprika, pepper and salt until finely chopped. Add the lemon juice and olive oil and blend until smooth.

Pour the piri-piri into an airtight container and store in the fridge until needed.

BBQ EXTRAS

Here are some brilliantly simple ideas to make your barbecue extra special.

- Chop sweetcorn cobs in half, cook on the barbecue until charred, then smother with butter and a shake of sea salt mixed with chilli flakes to taste.
- Halve red peppers and discard the seeds, brush with olive oil and leave to sizzle and soften over the hot coals.
- Place a medium-sized whole aubergine on the barbecue and turn at regular intervals until charred on the outside and soft on the inside. Cut the aubergine in half, scoop out the smoky flesh and mash with a couple of tablespoons of tahini, a good squeeze of lemon juice and seasoning to taste. Serve as a dip or smear on lamb burgers or vegetable brochettes.
- Slit large chillies down one side, remove the seeds and stuff with strips of seasoned mozzarella cheese. Cook until the chillies are charred and the mozzarella soft and gooey.
- Barbecued bananas and soft fruits round off a barbecue nicely. Place whole bananas (complete with skins) over the embers until the skin blackens and the flesh is soft (hedonists might like to slit the banana first and insert pieces of chocolate). Place ripe peach, nectarine or plum halves flesh side down on the grill, turn the fruit when it starts to soften and sprinkle liberally with soft brown sugar and ground cinnamon, pop a knob of butter into the hole and continue to cook until the butter melts and the sugar caramelizes.
- Don't forget the marshmallows to toast over the dying embers!

Polyprion oxygeneios
Normal max. size/weight: 180 cm/100 kgs

AU	Hapuku	GB	Groper, hapuku
	New Zealand groper	I	Cernia
D	Neuseeländischer		nuova zelandese
	Wrackbarsch	J	Ara
E	Cherna hapuku	NZ	Groper, hapuku
F	Cernier	US	Groper
	de Juan Fernández		

Sciaena gilberti
Normal max. size: 90 cm

AU	Croaker	GB	Curvina drum
F	Curvina pampera	US	Corvina
	Courbine blonde		

Squalus acanthias
Normal max. size/weight: 130 cm/9.1 kgs

AU	White-spotted	GB	Spiny dogfish
	dogfish, spurdog	I	Spinarolo
D	Gemeiner Dornhai,	J	Aburatsunozame
	Spurdai	KOB	Dum-bal-sang-eo
E	Tollo in cartan,	NZ	Southern spiny
	mielga, galludo		dogfish
	Aguillat commun	US	Spiny dogfish

Sebastes goodei
Normal max. size: 58 cm

E	Chancharro	GB	Chilipepper
	pimienta	US	Chilipepper
F	Sébaste piment		rockfish

Engraulis ringens
Normal max. size: 18 cm

AU	Anchovy	J	Aceitgo del Cile
E	Peru-sardelle	J	Jwashi
F	Anchoveta peruana	NZ	Anchovy
	Anchois du Pérou	US	Anchovy
GB	Peruvian anchovy,		
	anchoveta		

Thunnus maccoyii
Normal max. size/weight: 220 cm/400 kgs

AU	Bluefin,	I	Tonno
	southern tunny		Miami-maguro,
D	Südlicher Roter		indo-maguro
	Tun	J	Southern bluefin
E	Atún del sur		tuna
F	Thon rouge du sud		

Hippoglossus stenolepis
Normal max. size/weight: 260 cm/220 kgs

D	Pazifischer	GB	Pacific halibut
	Heilbutt	I	Halibut
E	Halibut		del Pacifico
	del Pacífico	J	Obyō
F	Flétan du Pacifique	US	Pacific halibut

Trachurus murphyi

E	Jurel	GB	Jurel, southern
	del Pacífico sur		jack mackerel
F	Chinchard jurel	US	Jack mackerel

Seriolella brama
Normal max. size: 70 cm

AU	Blue warehou	MAL	Aji-aji
D	Seriolella	NZ	Common warehou,
			warehou
J	Okihirasu, medai	US	Warehou

CATCH OF THE DAY

A collection of recipes that brings the seaside back home, breathing a breath of fresh sea air into the kitchen.

Sourcing the freshest possible fish is crucial. Having a local fishmonger you know and trust certainly makes the job a lot easier, but if you just follow a few basic rules you will be able to make your own informed decisions.

First check the fish's eyes: they must be bright and clear. Dull eyes sinking in the sockets should ring alarm bells.

A glossy sheen to the skin is always a good sign. If the skin has become opaque and sticky, walk on by.

Fresh fish always looks firm and plump. A limp, lifeless appearance is a definite no-no.

Pinky-red gills are a good indication of freshness. If the gills are grey and sticky, the fish has been sitting around too long.

One might expect that a fish should smell fishy – but on the contrary, a strong fishy aroma is a sure sign it is well past its sell-by date.

OATMEAL-COATED MACKEREL
WITH HONEY-CARAMELIZED ONIONS & APPLE

Wholesome oatmeal-coated oily fish, particularly popular in Scotland, are very easy to prepare, putting them top of the list for a no-nonsense first night home supper.

SERVES 2
Olive oil
1 medium red onion, thinly sliced
1 small sweet apple, cored, peeled and diced
1 garlic clove, crushed
Olive oil to fry
A pinch of cinnamon
A dash of cider vinegar
A tablespoon of honey
2 mackerel, filleted
2 tablespoons melted butter, plus extra to fry
A couple of handfuls of fine or medium oatmeal
Salt and freshly ground black pepper
Watercress, to serve

Coat the bottom of a frying pan with olive oil and fry the onion, apple and garlic until soft but not brown. Add a dash of cider vinegar and allow it to reduce by half before adding the cinnamon. Stir in the honey and continue to reduce, stirring constantly until the onion and apple caramelize.

Rinse the mackerel fillets in cold water and pat dry with kitchen paper. Brush both sides of the fish with melted butter and season to taste with salt and black pepper.

Line the bottom of a shallow dish with oatmeal, lay each mackerel fillet on top and firmly press into the oatmeal on both sides until well coated.

Add a generous knob of butter (and any remaining melted butter) to a heavy-bottomed frying pan, and heat the pan until the butter starts to foam.

Cook the coated fillets (flesh side down first) for a couple of minutes on both sides until the oatmeal becomes golden brown and crunchy.

Serve topped with the caramelized onion and apple, and a handful of watercress on the side.

SKATE WINGS WITH SAGE, BROWN BUTTER & CAPERS

Skate has firm white flesh that pulls easily away from the central cartilaginous skeleton. When buying skate, always check it is from a sustainable source. If in doubt, substitute lemon sole or large dabs. Serve with buttered wilted spinach and creamy mashed potato.

SERVES 2
2 medium skinless skate wings
2 tablespoons plain flour
75g/3oz butter
6 sage leaves
2 tablespoons salted capers, rinsed
Salt and freshly ground black pepper
A sprinkling of chopped parsley and lemon wedges, to serve

Rinse the skate wings in cold water and pat dry with kitchen paper.

Season the flour with salt (just a little as the capers are already salty) and freshly ground black pepper. Coat the skate wings with the seasoned flour and shake away any excess.

Heat half the butter in a large frying pan until it starts to foam. Add the skate wings and fry on both sides for 3–4 minutes (depending on how thick the skate is) until the pinkish flesh becomes white and the outside lightly browned. Remove from the pan and cover with foil to keep warm.

Melt the remaining butter in the pan, add the sage and gently bubble away until the butter turns caramel in colour (taking care not to burn it).

Add the capers and simmer for a minute before returning the fish briefly to the pan. Spoon the brown butter over the fish and serve immediately with a sprinkling of chopped parsley and a squeeze of lemon.

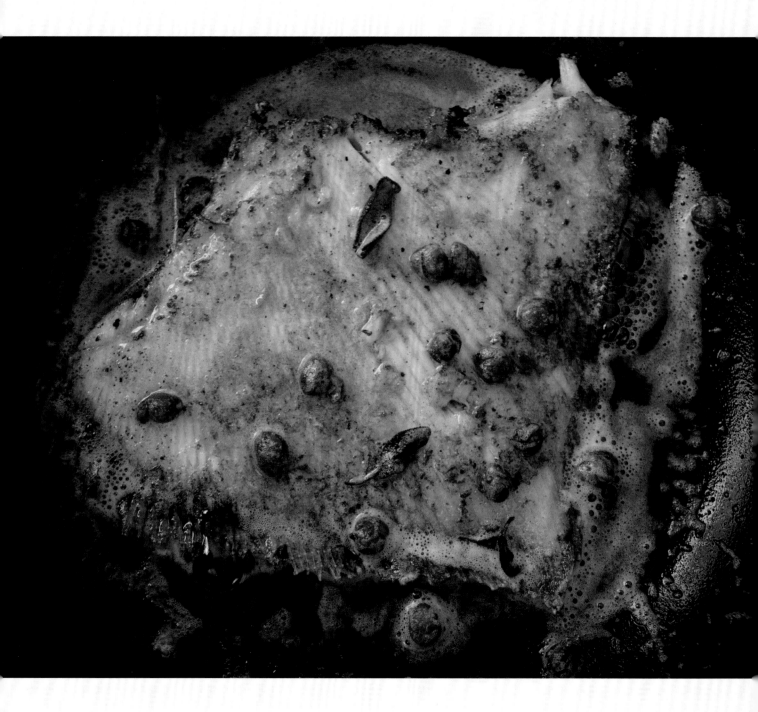

HADDOCK BAKED IN PAPER
WITH LEEKS, PEPPERS & ANCHOVY HERB BUTTER

———◆———

Cooking chunky fish fillets wrapped in a paper parcel seals in all the wonderful juices, keeping the flesh moist and flavoursome. To make anchovy herb butter follow the recipe on page 54, replacing the garlic with seven roughly chopped anchovy fillets.

SERVES 2
1 small leek, cleaned, trimmed and thinly sliced
1 pointed sweet red pepper, deseeded and thinly sliced
2 chunky haddock fillets (approximately 175g/6oz each)
2 dessertspoons anchovy herb butter
Salt and freshly ground black pepper

Preheat the oven to 220°C/425°F/gas mark 7.

Cut two generous squares of greaseproof paper (large enough to wrap the fish and vegetables loosely).

Place the sliced leek and pepper in the middle of each piece of greaseproof paper and lay the haddock fillets on top. Top each fillet with a dessertspoon of anchovy herb butter and season to taste (remember, anchovies are very salty, so be cautious about adding extra salt).

Wrap the greaseproof paper loosely over the fish and tightly fold the edges together to make a parcel.

Place the parcels on a baking tray and cook in the oven for 15 minutes.

PAN-FRIED POLLOCK WITH PANCETTA, FRESH PEAS & TARTARE SAUCE

Pollock makes a versatile and sustainable alternative to cod, and smoky pancetta and pimentón are perfect partners to its robust white flesh. To achieve nicely browned pancetta it's important to use chunky pollock fillets that require a longer cooking time.

SERVES 2
2 chunky pollock fillets (approximately 175g/6oz), skin removed
A light sprinkling of pimentón
4 slices pancetta, rind removed
2 sprigs thyme
Salt and freshly ground black pepper
Olive oil to fry
A generous tablespoon of butter
250g/9oz podded fresh peas lightly cooked
Tartare sauce (see page 74)

Season the pollock fillets with salt and black pepper to taste and sprinkle with a light dusting of pimentón.

Stretch each slice of pancetta by running the blunt side of a knife along its length, gently pulling as you do so. Wrap the stretched pancetta around the fish and tuck a sprig of thyme underneath.

Heat a generous splash of olive oil in a heavy-bottomed frying pan. Fry the fish on both sides until the pancetta is brown and the pollock is just cooked through.

Push the fish to the edge of the pan, add the butter and once melted add the cooked peas. Briefly turn the peas in the butter until well coated.

Pile the peas on a plate and top with the pollock. Serve immediately with a spoon of tartare sauce.

HOMEMADE TARTARE SAUCE

Where would we be without creamy, piquant tartare sauce to accompany fish? It's well worth taking the time to mix your own. It makes all the difference and any leftovers can be stored in the fridge for up to a week.

MAKES 150ml/¼ pint
150ml/¼ pint mayonnaise
1 heaped tablespoon capers,
   finely chopped
3 baby gherkins, finely chopped
1 teaspoon finely chopped tarragon
1 dessertspoon finely chopped
   curly parsley
A good squeeze of lemon juice
Salt and freshly ground black pepper
   to taste

Lightly whisk the mayonnaise with a fork until smooth and fluffy. Combine with the remaining ingredients and chill in the fridge until ready to serve.

BUTTERED SAMPHIRE

Thin-stemmed bright green samphire foraged from the coastal shoreline has a unique crisp succulent texture. Its salty intense flavour is a true taste of the sea. Fishmongers and some supermarkets sell this seaside rarity during samphire's relatively short growing season in July and August. Snap it up, it won't be around for long!

Samphire is a joy to cook: just plunge it into simmering water for a few minutes, or lightly steam. A little goes a long way – a modest handful per person is enough. Add to a seafood salad or simply dress with a knob of melted butter.

Wash the samphire thoroughly and cut away any barky stems. Bring a pan of water to a brisk simmer (salt is not necessary), drop the samphire into the water and cook for a maximum of two minutes. Drain well, add a generous knob of butter and gently turn the samphire in the butter as it melts.

WHOLE PLAICE BAKED WITH VINE TOMATOES, OLIVES & CRUSHED POTATOES

A bed of crushed potatoes soaks up the roast juices from the tomatoes, olives and plaice.

SERVES 2
2 medium-sized waxy potatoes
Olive oil
1 large whole plaice (approximately 900g/2lb, gutted with skin left on)
Butter
2 vines of cherry tomatoes on the vine (approximately 8 on each vine)
A small handful of black olives
1 large garlic clove, cut into slivers
3 sprigs of rosemary
Salt and freshly ground black pepper to taste

Preheat the oven to 200°C/400°F/gas mark 6.

Peel and quarter the potatoes and simmer in salted water until just soft. Drain the potatoes and lightly crush with the back of a fork until they start to break down.

Place the potatoes in the middle of a roasting tray (large enough to fit the fish) and drizzle with olive oil until well coated.

Rinse the plaice with cold water and pat dry with kitchen paper. Lay the fish on top of the crushed potatoes and dot with butter.

Place the strings of tomatoes alongside the fish and scatter the olives, garlic and rosemary evenly around. Drizzle everything generously with olive oil and season to taste.

Bake in the preheated oven for 15 minutes, then turn the oven temperature up to 220°C/425°F/gas mark 7 and cook for a further 10 minutes until the tomatoes are tender and starting to burst and the fish is moist and just cooked through.

POACHED LEMON SOLE IN A CREAMY SAFFRON & RAISIN SAUCE

An ancient culinary combination that's always in fashion. Serve with buttered, salty samphire when in season (see page 75).

This method also makes a great base for a herb sauce. Replace raisins and fennel seeds with a scattering of finely chopped fish-loving sorrel or dill, adding the herbs at the same time as the cream.

SERVES 2
2 good-sized lemon sole fillets
1 tablespoon butter
75ml/3 fl oz dry white wine
75ml/3 fl oz fish stock
1 heaped tablespoon golden raisins
2 bay leaves
4 black peppercorns
A good pinch of fennel seeds
A pinch of crushed saffron stamens
75ml/3 fl oz double cream
Salt

Preheat the oven to 190°C/375°F/gas mark 5.

Lay the sole in a roasting pan and dot with butter. Pour in the wine and fish stock and season with salt to taste. Add the raisins, bay leaves, peppercorns and fennel seeds.

Cover the pan with foil and cook in the preheated oven for 10 minutes, until the fish is just cooked through.

Carefully remove the fish from the pan, pop on to a warm plate and cover with kitchen foil to keep warm.

Place the roasting pan (complete with the fishy wine juices and raisins) on the stove top over a low heat. Add the saffron and simmer for a few minutes before adding the cream. Continue to cook over a low heat until the sauce thickens to the consistency of double cream.

Pour the sauce over the sole and serve immediately.

OR TRY DAB?

The much-underrated dab is a cheaper alternative to plaice or lemon sole. Its delicate soft flesh is perfect for baking on the bone. Dabs are the smallest of the flat fish family – choose the biggest you can find.

SEA BASS CAESAR SALAD WITH SORREL & SAMPHIRE

Samphire and lemony sorrel leaves topped with griddled sea bass, a tasty twist to a classic Caesar salad.

When samphire is out of season, you can substitute blanched asparagus tips or fine green beans. If you can't find sorrel, replace with mizuna, watercress or bitter endive leaves. You can use almost any fish fillets in this recipe, and if you find the prospect of raw egg scary, substitute a tablespoon of good-quality mayonnaise.

SERVES 2
2 thick slices of ciabatta or sourdough bread, cut into cubes
Olive oil
1 garlic clove, thinly sliced
1 Romaine heart, leaves separated and cut into 5cm/2 inch strips
A large handful of sorrel leaves
50g/2oz blanched samphire
Grated Parmesan to taste
2 sea bass fillets, skin on (approximately 175g/6oz each)

The dressing
1 garlic clove, crushed
1 medium free-range egg yolk
1 dessertspoon lemon juice
A good shake of Worcestershire sauce
3 tablespoons olive oil
Salt and freshly ground black pepper

Coat the bottom of a frying pan with olive oil and fry the cubed bread with the sliced garlic until golden and crunchy. Tip the croutons on to a plate and set to one side to cool.

Whisk the garlic, egg yolk, lemon juice and Worcestershire sauce in a small bowl until creamy. Slowly whisk in the olive oil in a steady stream. Season with salt and black pepper to taste.

Mix the salad leaves together and divide between two plates. Sprinkle the leaves with the blanched samphire and croutons.

Brush the sea bass fillets with olive oil and season to taste. Heat a ridged griddle pan until smoking hot and cook the fillets on both sides until seared on the outside and cooked through.

Drizzle the salad with dressing to taste, sprinkle with a generous amount of grated Parmesan and place the sea bass fillets on top.

RED MULLET COOKED TAJINE-STYLE WITH CHERMOULA

Chermoula is a classic Moroccan marinade for fish. It can be used to coat grilled fish or fish cooked in a tajine. If you are lucky enough to own a tajine, fantastic, otherwise a large, heavy-bottomed frying pan with a fitted lid works just as well. Rustle up a tomato salad to accompany.

SERVES 2
2 red mullet (approximately 300g/11oz each in weight),
   gutted and descaled
1 medium red onion, finely sliced
1 baking potato, peeled and thinly sliced
½ green pepper, thinly sliced
2 medium plum tomatoes, sliced
5 artichoke hearts, cut in half
1 preserved lemon, quartered, or 1 fresh lemon, quartered and blanched
A handful of finely chopped flat-leaf parsley
2 tablespoons olive oil

The chermoula
1 teaspoon ground cumin
1 teaspoon ground coriander
1 teaspoon ground paprika
¼ teaspoon cracked black pepper
A pinch of saffron
2 garlic cloves, roughly chopped
Small handful coriander leaves, finely chopped
2 tablespoons olive oil
A good squeeze of lemon juice
Salt to taste

To make the chermoula, whizz the marinade ingredients in a food processor until a wet paste forms.

Score both sides of the red mullet with a sharp knife at 2-cm/¾-inch intervals, rub half the chermoula into the skin.

Layer the onion, potato, pepper and tomato in the bottom of your chosen cooking vessel. Scatter with the artichoke hearts, preserved lemon and chopped parsley.

Mix the remaining chermoula with the olive oil and four tablespoons of water. Drizzle evenly over the vegetables, cover the pan and gently simmer on a low heat for twenty minutes.

Lay the red mullet on top of the vegetables, cover the pan, and cook for a further twenty minutes, until the fish flakes easily when a knife is inserted in the thickest part.

TOMATO SALAD

Top a bed of rocket leaves with thick-cut plum tomato slices, sprinkle with finely chopped red onion and olives and drizzle with seasoned olive oil whisked with a good squeeze of lemon juice.

A DOVER SOLE SUPPER

Dover sole has such a light, delicate taste, it would be a crime to smother it with heavy flavours. Baking whole in foil enhances the subtle taste and texture of the fish. Serve with lightly cooked purple sprouting or young stem broccoli. If Dover sole is unavailable, opt for lemon sole or plaice.

Ask your fishmonger to remove the Dover sole's thick top skin.

SERVES 2
2 medium-sized Dover sole (approximately 350g/12oz each,
  before skinning)
Olive oil
Butter
A few sprigs of thyme
Lemon juice
Salt and freshly ground black pepper

Preheat the oven to 220°C/425°F/gas mark 7.

Cut two good-sized oblongs of kitchen foil (large enough to wrap the fish loosely and allow steam to circulate).

Lay each fish in the centre of one of the pieces of foil and drizzle with olive oil. Add a couple of knobs of butter, a sprig of thyme, a squeeze of lemon and season to taste. Wrap the fish loosely with the foil, making sure there are no holes in the seal.

Place the fish parcel on a baking tray and cook in the preheated oven for ten minutes.

Serve drizzled with the cooking juices from the foil.

SMOKED HADDOCK CHOWDER

—◆—

Creamy, chunky smoked haddock chowder makes a comforting one-pot supper after a day on the beach. If you are missing your greens, add a handful or two of roughly chopped baby-leaf spinach at the same time as the parsley.

SERVES 2
200g/7oz undyed smoked haddock
3 black peppercorns
2 bay leaves
1 heaped tablespoon butter
2 shallots, finely chopped
2 rashers streaky bacon, sliced
1 small leek, cleaned, trimmed and thinly sliced
1 baking potato, peeled and diced
1 sprig thyme
225ml/8fl oz full-fat milk
55ml/2fl oz single cream
A couple of sprigs of flat-leaf parsley, finely chopped
Salt and freshly ground black pepper
A small bunch of chives, roughly chopped, to garnish

Lay the smoked haddock fillets in the bottom of a frying pan. Pour 150ml/¼ pint boiling water over the top and add the peppercorns and bay leaves. Bring the pan to the boil then reduce the heat and simmer for a couple of minutes, until the fish is just cooked through. Remove the fish from the pan and retain the cooking water. When the fish is cool enough to touch break into chunks, discarding any bones you come across.

Melt the butter in a heavy-bottomed pan, add the onion, leek and bacon and cook over a low heat until the vegetables are soft but not brown. Stir in the potatoes until they are well coated in butter.

Strain the retained cooking water into the pan and add the milk and the thyme. Cover the pan and gently simmer until the potatoes are soft.

Using a potato masher, roughly mash the potatoes until they start to break down but still retain some texture.

Add the cream and gently simmer for a couple of minutes before stirring in the parsley and haddock. Cook for a further minute or so, until the fish is heated through – any longer and you run the risk of its becoming rubbery. Finally, season to taste, ladle into bowls and garnish with chopped chives.

SEASHELLS

Packed full of goodness and flavour, these tasty treasures are easier to prepare than you might think. Whether you are a seasoned shellfish eater or a nervous novice, these recipes will simplify the classics and offer food for thought.

OYSTERS, MUSSELS & SCALLOPS

Oysters and mussels in the shell must be alive and kicking immediately before they are prepared. A firmly clamped shell is a good indication that all's well, but there are exceptions to the rule. Tap any open shells: if they fail to close, discard immediately along with any broken or damaged shells.

It is also preferable to buy scallops live in the shell. The fishmonger will be happy to clean them for you. Keep the shells: they make very useful cooking pots on the barbecue or under the grill and look rather glamorous on the plate. If scallops in the shell are hard to source, choose prepared scallops with plump white flesh and no visible ragged edges.

To store shellfish, discard any sealed plastic wrapping, tip into a bowl and cover with a cloth. Place the bowl in the lower part of the fridge until ready to use.

Take the time to wash mussels and oysters thoroughly. A nail brush is the right size to scrub away any remnants of stubborn sand.

Cooking shellfish is straightforward. The most important tip is only to cook the shells for a few minutes. Longer than that and the soft flesh becomes tough and rubbery.

When seasoning shellfish with salt, start with a modest shake; they are already salty from the sea.

MUSSELS COOKED THREE WAYS

To prepare mussels, use a stout knife to scape away any stubborn barnacles clinging to the shell and pull away the beard on the side of the shell. Discard any mussels with broken shells or that fail to close when tapped. Give the mussels a good wash in cold water (crunching on gritty mussels is no fun) and they are ready to go.

Place a large empty bowl in the middle of the table to collect the empty shells and prepare a small finger bowl of warm water with a slice of lemon per person. Always discard any mussels that are still closed after cooking.

Empty mussel shells double up brilliantly as tweezers to extract cooked mussels and a spoon to scoop mouthfuls of sauce.

THAI MUSSELS WITH LEMONGRASS & COCONUT MILK

SERVES 4
2 tablespoons sunflower oil
1 small onion, finely chopped
3 garlic cloves, crushed
2–3 thinly sliced red chilli
1 × 400g/14oz tin coconut milk
110ml/4 floz fish stock
4 lime leaves, thinly sliced
2 thinly sliced lemongrass stalks
Juice of a lime
2 kg/4½ lb prepared mussels
A handful of coriander leaves, roughly chopped

Heat the oil in a large saucepan, add the onion, garlic and chilli, cover the pan and sweat the vegetables over a low heat until soft but not brown.

Add the coconut milk, fish stock, lime juice, lime leaves and lemongrass and simmer for a couple of minutes before adding the mussels. Cover the pan and cook over a high heat for 3–4 minutes, shaking the pan, until the mussels open. Add the chopped coriander just before serving.

MUSSELS WITH CIDER, LEEK & BACON

Still scrumpy cider adds a fruity roundness to this buttery cider sauce. For a fiery kick, throw in a couple of sliced red chillies!

SERVES 4
3 tablespoons butter
110g/4oz diced pancetta
1 medium leek, cleaned and sliced
1 small red onion, thinly sliced
2 garlic cloves, crushed
200ml/7fl oz still dry scrumpy cider
110ml/4 fl oz hot vegetable or fish stock
2kg/4½ lb prepared mussels
A good handful of flat-leaf parsley, finely chopped

Melt the butter in a large saucepan, add the pancetta and cook until it starts to brown. Add the leek, onion and garlic, cover the pan and sweat together until the vegetables are soft but not brown.

Tip the prepared mussels into the pan, pour in the cider and let it splutter and reduce a little before adding the stock. Cover the pan and cook over a high heat, shaking the pan, for 3–4 minutes, until the mussels open. Add the parsley and serve immediately. Discard any mussels that fail to open.

TOMATO & BASIL MUSSELS

SERVES 4

3 tablespoons olive oil
1 medium red onion, diced
2 garlic cloves, crushed
1 small glass dry white wine
1½ tins chopped tomatoes (400g/14oz size)
2 kg/4½ lb prepared mussels
2 heaped tablespoons butter
A handful of basil leaves, roughly chopped
A handful of parsley, finely chopped (set a little
  aside to garnish)
Salt and freshly ground black pepper to taste
A good squeeze of lemon juice

Heat the olive oil in a large saucepan, add the onion and garlic and fry until soft but not brown.

Pour in the white wine and let it splutter away until reduced by half. Add the chopped tomatoes, herbs and a good squeeze of lemon juice, and simmer until the sauce has thickened and the oil has returned. Stir in the butter and adjust the seasoning with salt and black pepper to taste.

Add the mussels, cover the pan, and cook over a high heat for 3–4 minutes, shaking the pan, until the mussels open. Sprinkle with the remaining chopped parsley before serving.

OYSTERS THREE WAYS

Oysters are a real delicacy, sweet and briny, a true taste of the sea. They do however tend to separate people into two camps, like or loathe! Sceptics – give them a try and you just might find yourself converted by the charm of a freshly shucked oyster with a squeeze of lemon or a dash of shallot vinaigrette, or grilled with buttery breadcrumbs.

Time is of the essence when cooking oysters – a few minutes is all they need. The oyster is ready when the flesh starts to looks creamy. Don't delay in serving, the oyster will continue to cook in the hot juices. A piece of scrunched tin foil placed under each shell is indispensable if you want to keep oysters flat on a grill pan.

HOW TO SHUCK AN OYSTER

You have to take a strong-arm approach to opening oysters – but investing in a sturdy shucking knife certainly makes the job a lot easier. Give the oysters a good scrub under running water and discard any shells that are damaged or remain open. Using an old clean tea towel, firmly hold an oyster cup-side down with the pointed hinge facing towards you. Fully insert the shucking knife into the hinge and twist the blade until the hinge releases. Open the shell (taking care to keep the shell flat to retain the juices) slide the knife under the oyster and cut through the foot to release the oyster from the shell. Finally remove any bits of shell that have broken away.

If you can resist immediately adding a squeeze of lemon and downing the oyster in one go, display the shucked shells in the traditional way on a bed of crushed ice with plenty of lemon wedges. Shallot vinaigrette makes a classic dressing and a shake of Tabasco adds a spicy twist.

SCALLOPED OYSTERS

—◆—

Grilled oysters topped with cayenne-spiked buttered breadcrumbs.

To make breadcrumbs, remove the crusts from a large chunk of dry white bread, cut into cubes and whizz in a food processor until finely chopped. Any excess breadcrumbs can be frozen.

MAKES 12 OYSTERS
75g/3oz homemade breadcrumbs
3 tablespoons butter
¼–½ teaspoon cayenne pepper
1 tablespoon finely chopped chives
12 shucked oysters left in the cupped half of the shell
Lemon wedges to serve

Melt the butter in a frying pan, stir in the breadcrumbs and cook over a low heat until the breadcrumbs turn golden brown. Stir in the cayenne and chives.

Tip away half the juice from each shucked oyster and cover with a spoonful of fried breadcrumbs. Place under a hot grill (not too close to the grill) and cook for 2–3 minutes until the breadcrumbs are crunchy and the oyster looks creamy.

Serve with a squeeze of lemon.

CLASSIC SHALLOT VINAIGRETTE

Chop the shallots as finely as you possibly can before combining with the vinaigrette, spoon to taste on to a shucked oyster and down in one (or chew).

FOR APPROXIMATELY 12 OYSTERS
100ml/4floz red wine vinegar
1 tablespoon freshly squeezed lemon juice
1 teaspoon caster sugar
1 banana shallot, very finely chopped
Freshly ground black pepper

Stir the red wine vinegar, lemon juice and caster sugar together until the sugar has dissolved. Add the chopped shallots and season with a good grind of black pepper.

OYSTERS GRILLED WITH CREAM & PARMESAN

Silky soft oysters, warm cream and the crunch of grilled Parmesan.

MAKES 12 OYSTERS
12 shucked oysters left in the cupped half of the shell
65ml/2½ fl oz double cream
4 tablespoons grated Parmesan cheese
Freshly ground black pepper
Lemon wedges to serve

Tip away half the liquid from each oyster before placing on a grill pan. Add a teaspoon of cream to each oyster, top with a teaspoon of grated Parmesan and season with black pepper.

Carefully slide the pan under a hot grill and cook the oysters for 2–3 minutes, until the flesh turns creamy. Serve immediately with a squeeze of lemon.

SCALLOPS THREE WAYS

Scallops are at their very best when quickly seared in a hot pan, caramelizing the outside but leaving the middle slightly opaque.

Scallops sold in the shell will still have the roe attached. Ideally the roe should look well rounded and bright orange – if it is shrivelled, discard before cooking.

These recipes comfortably feed four people as a main course. Alternatively, you can halve the quantity and serve as a starter. If the scallops are particularly plump, they can be cut in half.

SEARED SCALLOPS WITH SOY SAUCE & GINGER

Soy sauce and ginger marry perfectly with seared scallops. Serve with wilted spinach and barely cooked fine green beans or asparagus.

SERVES 4
16 scallops
4cm/1½ inch piece ginger root, grated
3 tablespoons light soy sauce
2 teaspoons sesame oil
1 teaspoon clear honey
A splash of sunflower oil
Coriander leaves, to garnish

Rinse the scallops in cold water and pat dry with kitchen paper.

Whisk the ginger, soy sauce, sesame oil and honey in a small bowl until well combined.

Add a splash of sunflower oil to a heavy-bottomed frying pan. Using a piece of kitchen paper, wipe the oil over the bottom of the pan until evenly coated.

Heat the pan until the oil starts to smoke, add the scallops and sear on both sides for 1 minute. Pour in the soy mixture and allow it to splutter away for a minute or so (turning the scallops halfway through), until the scallops are just cooked through.

Serve sprinkled with coriander leaves.

SCALLOPS WITH CRISPY FRIED PARMA HAM, CAULIFLOWER PUREE & THYME BUTTER

If you have kept the scallop shells, scrub thoroughly in hot water before serving this dish layered inside the shell.

SERVES 4
16 scallops
½ medium cauliflower, cut into small florets
55ml/2 fl oz double cream
3 tablespoons butter
Olive oil
8 slices Parma ham, cut in half
2 sprigs thyme
Salt and freshly ground black pepper to taste

Rinse the scallops in cold water and pat dry with kitchen paper.

To make the cauliflower purée, cook the florets in simmering water until soft. Drain well and allow to cool a little before blending in a food processor with cream and a generous tablespoon of butter until smooth. Transfer the purée to a small saucepan and season to taste.

Fry the Parma ham (in two batches) in a splash of olive oil until golden brown and crinkled. Drain the ham on kitchen paper while it becomes crispy.

Heat the remaining butter in the same frying pan. When it starts to foam, add the thyme and the scallops (eight at a time). Cook the scallops for 1–2 minutes on each side, until they are caramelized on the outside and just cooked through the middle.

Give the cauliflower purée a quick burst of heat before dividing between the scallop shells. Top the purée with a scallop, spoon over any buttery juices left in the pan and cover with a slice of crispy Parma ham.

SCALLOP PATTIES WITH CHILLI DIPPING SAUCE

Crunchy breadcrumb-coated scallops dipped into homemade chilli sauce make a moreish starter. For a larger meal, serve with a salad of mixed peppery leaves.

SERVES 4
16 scallops
1 large free-range egg
110g/4oz homemade breadcrumbs
Grated zest of a large lemon
1 tablespoon finely chopped parsley
Plain flour
Salt and freshly ground black pepper
Butter to fry

Dipping sauce
2 medium-sized red chillies, finely chopped
1 medium-sized green chilli, finely chopped
4 tablespoons clear honey
3 tablespoons rice wine vinegar
3 dessertspoons hot water
1 tablespoon lime juice

Combine the dipping sauce ingredients in a small pan and simmer over a low heat until the sauce becomes syrupy. Season to taste with salt and black pepper.

Rinse the scallops in cold water and pat dry with kitchen paper.

Beat the egg with salt and black pepper to taste until well mixed. Combine the breadcrumbs, lemon zest and chopped parsley in a shallow bowl and line a separate shallow bowl with plain flour.

Coat each scallop in plain flour, followed by beaten egg and finally breadcrumbs.

Heat a generous knob of butter in a non-stick frying pan. When the butter starts to foam add the scallops and cook in two batches until the breadcrumbs become golden brown (adding extra butter when necessary).

Serve immediately with chilli dipping sauce on the side.

CRAB & LOBSTER

While away a lazy lunch feasting on a whole freshly cracked crab or lobster. Crab and lobster are generally sold pre-cooked, which simplifies things for the squeamish. To avoid 'watery' crab, where the body is filled with water rather than precious meat, lift the crab and check it feels heavy. If handling the crab is out of the question, choose one with a weathered, barnacled shell and well worn serrations to the claws. When buying cooked lobster, look for shiny eyes, firm flesh and a curled tail.

HOW TO CRACK A CRAB & DRESS A LOBSTER

Once you have selected your crab, it's time to get cracking. A large crab should yield around 300g/11oz of meat. There are several useful tools available to help remove every last scrap – a long picking stick is particularly useful to winkle out white meat. Claw crackers are also handy; however, a sturdy pair of nutcrackers also does the job.

There are two approaches to picking meat from the crab – you can either eat as you go, or meticulously remove the meat and 'dress' the crab shell. Always be on the lookout for small bits of shell that sneak through the picking process.

Place the crab shell side down on a board and twist the legs and claws from the body. Separate the underside from the shell by inserting the back of a spoon into the gap just below the eyes and prising apart. Discard the stomach sack, mouth and 'dead man's fingers' (the inedible off-white gills). Spoon out the dark meat and delve into the nooks and crannies of the shell to find all the hidden white meat. Finally, crack the claws and the legs to access the most highly prized white meat. To 'dress' a crab, rinse the shell, place the brown meat down the centre and fill the sides with white meat.

Dressing a cooked lobster is much simpler. All you have to do is halve the lobster, remove a few bits and pieces and crack the claws. Place the lobster underside downwards on a chopping board. Cut through the head section using a long sharp knife, starting from the point where the head joins the tail and following the central line. Complete the job by cutting the tail in half from the middle outwards. Remove the stomach sack and the grey gills from the head section, and tease out the black intestinal tract that runs the length of the tail. Crack the claws with a pair of claw crackers and dig in.

Fresh crab or lobster needs little more than a dollop of homemade mayonnaise and a squeeze of fresh lemon juice.

FOOLPROOF MAYONNAISE

Only thick, glossy homemade mayonnaise will do for luxurious fresh crab and lobster. Add a sprinkling of chopped herbs, crushed garlic or a shake of Tabasco, or serve just as it comes.

To prevent the mayonnaise curdling, add the oil in a slow, steady stream and always take care to whisk continuously.

MAKES 275ml/½ pint
2 large free-range egg yolks
1 teaspoon Dijon or English mustard
275ml/½ pint rapeseed oil
2 tablespoons lemon juice
Salt and freshly ground black pepper

Whisk the egg yolks and mustard with an electric hand whisk (or in a food processor) until light and fluffy.

Whisking constantly, add the oil in a slow, steady stream, until the mixture thickens.

Whisk in the lemon juice and season with salt and black pepper to taste.

DEVILLED CRAB

———◆———

Spicy devilled crab served with watercress and hot buttered toast makes a perfect light lunch.

SERVES 4
Brown and white meat picked from a large whole crab
  (or a ready dressed crab)
4 tablespoons mayonnaise
Juice and zest of a lime
A shake of Worcestershire sauce
1 red chilli, finely chopped
A small bunch of coriander leaves, roughly chopped
Salt and black pepper to taste

To serve
Watercress drizzled with a dressing made from the juice of a small lime
  whisked with 4 tablespoons of olive oil and seasoning to taste.
Thin slices of hot buttered wholemeal toast

Mix the brown and white meat together in a bowl.

In a separate bowl, whisk the mayonnaise with the lime juice and Worcestershire sauce until smooth, stir in the chopped chilli and coriander and season to taste.

Combine the mayonnaise with the crab meat and sprinkle on top of the dressed watercress leaves. Serve with slices of hot buttered toast.

CRAB LINGUINE

Pasta stretches precious crab meat without compromising on taste.

SERVES 4
350g/12oz linguine
3 tablespoons olive oil, plus extra to serve
2 cloves garlic, finely chopped
1 large red chilli, finely chopped
110ml/4fl oz double cream
A good squeeze of lemon juice
A small bunch of parsley, finely chopped
Brown and white meat picked from a large whole crab (or a dressed crab)
Salt and freshly ground black pepper to taste

Bring a large pan of salted water to the boil, add the linguine and cook until al dente. Drain the pasta, return to the pan and drizzle with a tablespoon of olive oil.

Fry the garlic and chopped chilli in the remaining olive oil until soft but not brown. Stir in the cream, along with a good squeeze of lemon juice and the chopped parsley. Gently simmer for a minute before adding the crab meat.

Combine the crab mixture with the linguine over a low heat until the pasta is well coated with sauce and heated through.

Drizzle with extra olive oil just before serving.

THE BEST CRAB SANDWICH

Crab sandwiches are a real luxury. When you eat them by the seaside, the memory of fresh bread generously filled with picked crab lingers long after returning home.

MAKES 4 ROUNDS
8 medium-sliced pieces of crusty bread
Soft unsalted butter
4 tablespoons mayonnaise
Freshly picked brown and white crab meat from a large crab
    (or a dressed crab)
A shake of Worcestershire sauce
Lemon juice
Salt and ground white pepper
A small handful of parsley leaves, finely chopped

Butter the bread and thinly spread four of the slices with half the mayonnaise

Whisk the remaining mayonnaise with a shake of Worcestershire sauce and a squeeze of lemon juice. Stir in the brown meat and season to taste with salt and white pepper.

Combine the white meat with the finely chopped parsley, a squeeze of lemon and salt and pepper to taste.

Spread the four buttered slices of bread with the brown meat and cover with white meat.

Place the remaining slices of bread (mayonnaise side down) on top and gently press together.

Cut the sandwiches into triangles.

GRILLED LOBSTER WITH GARLIC BUTTER

Fresh lobster is such a treat, it seems a shame to overwhelm it with rich sauces. However, bubbling hot garlic butter makes a fitting partner.

Dot each lobster half with garlic butter to taste (see page 54) and cook under a hot grill until the butter melts and the lobster meat is golden brown.

ICES & MILKSHAKES

A visit to the seaside wouldn't be complete without a super-sized ice cream. It raises a smile on a cloudy day and when the sun shines it's definitely the icing on the cake. Homemade ice cream is a lot of fun to make and passes the taste test every time. You can experiment with your favourite flavours using the cheat's method or, if you are an ice cream purist, stick to the traditional route. When the freezer is chock-a-block with homemade ice cream you can reward yourself with a sandcastle-sized sundae or an ice-cold milk shake!

ICE CREAM GALORE!

Ice cream is traditionally made from an egg custard base. This is what creates the characteristic rich creamy texture we all know and love. Once the custard is made, you can let your imagination go wild with exciting flavour combinations; simply fold your favourites into the custard mixture before freezing. Here are some ideas to get you started.

FREEZING ICE CREAM THE TRADITIONAL WAY

If you are the proud owner of an ice cream maker, freezing a custard base is very straightforward – just pour the custard into the machine and follow the maker's instructions! The machine does all the work for you, constantly churning the custard as it freezes to create an ice-free smooth-textured ice cream. When using an ice cream maker, remember not to add chunky ingredients that break up easily until the end of the churning time.

Don't want to invest in an ice cream maker? Then transfer the chilled custard into a shallow freezer-proof container with a fitted lid and pop the tub in the freezer. After about an hour, when the custard starts to freeze around the edges, use a fork to break up the ice and whisk it into the ice cream. This process prevents the ice cream becoming crystalline, and must be repeated a couple more times before the ice cream is completely frozen. Expect this to take about six hours (although freezers do vary). For a nice soft scoop, place the ice cream in the fridge twenty minutes before serving.

VANILLA AND ROSE ICE CREAM

Old-fashioned vanilla is always a treat. Add scented rose water and it becomes a Turkish delight.

MAKES 700ml/1¼ pint
275ml/½ pint full-fat milk
275ml/½ pint double cream
1 vanilla pod, slit
4 large free-range egg yolks
110g/4oz castor sugar
4 tablespoons rose water

Pour the milk and cream into a saucepan, add the seeds scraped from inside the vanilla pod and warm together until bubbles start to form around the edge of the pan. Remove the pan from the heat and allow the mixture to cool while you prepare the egg base (if the mixture is too hot the eggs will curdle).

Beat the egg yolks and caster sugar with a hand whisk until the sugar crystals have dissolved and the mixture is light and fluffy. Gradually whisk in the warm milk in a steady stream. Pour the mixture into a clean saucepan. Gently cook the custard over a low heat, stirring constantly with a wooden spoon, until it thickens enough to coat the back of the spoon.

Pour the custard into a bowl, add the rose water and set aside until cool. Chill the cooled custard in the fridge for half an hour, then either pour into an ice cream maker and follow the maker's instructions or transfer into a shallow freezer-proof container and follow the method on page 122.

CHILLI CHOCOLATE ICE CREAM

Hot and cooling all at the same time! If a mellow spicy undertone isn't to your taste, stick to regular dark chocolate – or maybe chocolate with a hint of ginger or orange?

MAKES A GENEROUS 700ml/1¼ pint
275ml/½ pint full-fat milk
275ml/½ pint double cream
4 medium free-range egg yolks
110g/4oz caster sugar
100g/3½ oz dark chilli chocolate
    (preferably 70% cocoa solids),
    finely chopped
1 heaped tablespoon cocoa powder

Make the custard as described on page 125, omitting the vanilla and rose water. Whisk the chocolate and the cocoa powder into the hot custard until the chocolate has completely melted and the mixture is smooth. Allow to cool and churn the mixture in an ice cream maker or place in the freezer and continue as described on page 122.

SOFT FRUIT ICE CREAMS

In the height of summer, when soft fruit is bountiful, sweet fruity ice creams are a must. Blend 350g/12oz ripe strawberries or raspberries in a food processor with a tablespoon of icing sugar until smooth. If you object to pips, sieve the purée through a fine mesh before combining with the hot custard mixture (or cheat's no-churn ice cream, page 128). Little more is needed; a generous tablespoon of balsamic vinegar always complements strawberry purée, while a teaspoon of vanilla extract enhances raspberry.

For tarter fruit, such as rhubarb, gooseberries, plums, blackcurrants or blackberries, cook the prepared fruit with a tablespoon of water and caster sugar to taste before blending.

CHEAT'S NO-CHURN METHOD

A gloriously swift method that miraculously creates a soft, smooth ice cream without cooking or churning. Condensed milk is the secret ingredient that makes it all possible and as the thick milk is already sweetened, there's no need even to add sugar. The no-churn method is particularly useful when making ripple-effect ice creams or using ingredients that break up when churned.

MAKES 500ml/18fl oz
200ml/7fl oz condensed milk
275ml/½ pint double cream
1 teaspoon vanilla extract

Whip the condensed milk, cream and vanilla extract together with a hand whisk until soft peaks form. Add any additional flavours at this point and scoop the mixture into a freezer-proof container.

Cover the ice cream and place in the freezer until the mixture is completely frozen. This usually takes six to seven hours, but every freezer is different.

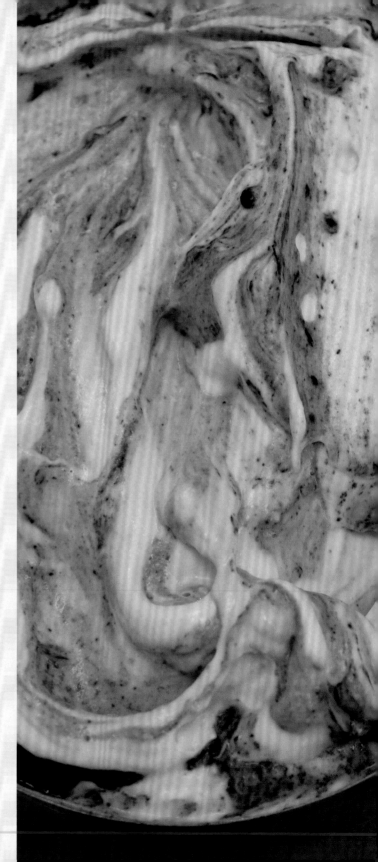

BLACKBERRY RIPPLE ICE CREAM

Blackberries make a dramatic, fragrant ripple. You can use the same method and quantity of soft fruit to concoct seasonal variations. Raspberries and blueberries ripple beautifully: scatter a handful of whole fruit into the mixture at the same time as the purée. Gooseberries add a tart zing, and you can complement the fruit by sweetening with elderflower cordial to taste. Add a dash of port to cranberry purée, kirsch to blackcurrant, or a sprinkle of ground ginger to plum.

MAKES 700ml/1¼ pint
Gently simmer 200g/7oz of prepared blackberries with two tablespoons of water and caster sugar to taste until the fruit is just soft. Blend the cooked fruit in a food processor until a purée forms (pass through a fine sieve for a pip-free purée) and leave to cool.

Whip up the cheat's no-churn ice cream base and scoop into a freezer-proof tub. Spoon dessertspoons of the puree randomly over the top of the ice cream and lightly stir to create a ripple effect. Cover the ice cream and place in the freezer until frozen through.

TOASTED ALMOND & RUM DULCE DE LECHE RIPPLE

Dulce de leche is a thick, unctuous caramel sauce that is available in jars from good food stores and supermarkets.

Toast 50g/2oz roughly chopped whole almonds in a dry pan over a medium heat until golden brown. Combine 5 tablespoons of dulce de leche with 2 tablespoons of rum. Sprinkle the cheat's ice cream with the toasted almonds and dribble the rum dulce de leche over the top, gently folding into the ice cream to create a ripple effect. Cover the ice cream and place in the freezer until completely frozen.

FABULOUS FLAVOURS

Stuck for ideas? Choose from these fabulous flavours: crushed peanut brittle or chocolate-coated honeycomb, finely chopped crystallized stem ginger, mini marshmallows, lemon curd, bite-sized pieces of white chocolate and whole raspberries, raisins soaked in rum, chopped pistachios with a good pinch of ground cardamom, a couple of strong espresso shots (or a heaped tablespoon of strong instant coffee dissolved in a little warm water) and a dash of coffee liqueur, a handful of finely chopped fresh mint leaves and good-quality dark chocolate.

SINFUL SUNDAE SAUCES

Homemade sundae sauces transform ice cream into something rather spectacular. Serve warm from the pan or allow to cool. Each recipe serves 4–6 depending on how much you like to douse! Stored in the fridge the sauces keep for up to a week, but rich chocolate and caramel maple sauce will thicken – to loosen again, warm with a splash of cream.

RICH CHOCOLATE SAUCE

110g/4oz good-quality dark chocolate (preferably with minimum 70% cocoa solids)
finely chopped 225ml/8 fl oz single cream
1 tablespoon clear honey
A modest knob of butter

Place the chopped chocolate and double cream in a small pan. Warm together over a low heat (stirring constantly) until the chocolate melts and the sauce is completely smooth.

Off the heat, add the honey and butter and stir together until the butter melts and the sauce looks glossy.

CARAMEL MAPLE SAUCE

—◀▶—

75g/3oz unsalted butter
75g/3oz soft brown sugar
25g/1oz maple syrup
110ml/4fl oz double cream

Place the butter, sugar and maple syrup in a small heavy-bottomed pan. Warm over a low heat, stirring constantly, until the butter and sugar have completely melted. Gently simmer for a couple of minutes before whisking in the cream. Bring the sauce back to a simmer and continue to cook for a further couple of minutes. Remove the pan from the heat and allow to cool a little before pouring into a container. The sauce will thicken as it cools.

SWEET STRAWBERRY SAUCE

—◀▶—

275g/10oz strawberries, hulled and quartered
3 tablespoons caster sugar
1 teaspoon vanilla extract
110ml/4fl oz water

Place the prepared strawberries, caster sugar and vanilla extract in a small pan, add the water and warm together over a low heat until the sugar melts. Bring the pan to a simmer and cook for a few minutes, until the strawberries soften.

Allow to cool slightly before blending in a food processor until smooth. Sieve to remove the pips if you wish.

SUMPTUOUS SUNDAES

Truly scrumptious retro-style ice cream sundaes.

CARAMELIZED BANANA SPLIT

MAKES 4
2 good tablespoons butter
2 tablespoons clear honey
¼ teaspoon ground cinnamon
4 ripe bananas, peeled and cut in half lengthwise
8 scoops toasted almond and rum dolce de leche ice cream
275ml/¼ pint double cream, whipped until thick
Rich chocolate and caramel maple sauce to taste
A small handful of chopped walnuts

Melt the butter in a frying pan and stir in the honey and cinnamon. Add the banana halves and cook for a couple of minutes on each side until soft and caramelized.

Lay each banana in a dish and top with two scoops of toasted almond and rum dolce de leche ice cream. Pipe whipped cream on top and drizzle with chocolate and caramel maple sauce to taste. Decorate with a sprinkling of toasted chopped hazelnuts.

SUMMER BERRY KNICKERBOCKER GLORY

MAKES 4

A handful each of strawberries, fresh cherries,
   raspberries and blueberries
8 scoops vanilla and rose ice cream
Sweet strawberry sauce to taste
150ml/¼ pint double cream, whipped until thick
Strawberries to decorate

Hull and quarter the strawberries and cut the
cherries in half (taking care to discard the stones).
Combine with the remaining fruit and divide
between four tall sundae glasses.

Dollop two scoops of vanilla and rose ice cream
on top and drizzle with sweet strawberry sauce
to taste. Top with a swirl of whipped cream and
decorate with a whole strawberry and an extra
drizzle of sauce.

POACHED PEACH MELBA

SERVES 4

4 medium-sized ripe peaches
200ml/7fl oz rosé wine (or cranberry juice)
200ml/7fl oz water
75g/3oz caster sugar
2 tablespoons honey
1 vanilla pod, slit
225g/8oz raspberries, plus a handful extra to
    decorate
8 scoops vanilla ice cream

Cut the peaches in half and discard the stones.

Pour the rosé wine and water into a saucepan large enough to fit all the peach halves. Stir in the sugar, the honey and the seeds scraped from the vanilla pod. Warm the pan over a low heat until the sugar dissolves, then increase the heat and briskly simmer until the mixture starts to look syrupy. Lay the peach halves in the syrup and simmer for a few minutes on each side until just soft. Remove the peaches and set aside.

Tip the raspberries into a bowl and pour 150ml/¼ pint of the hot syrup left in the pan over the top. Leave to stand for a minute, then pass through a fine sieve to make a sauce.

To assemble the peach melbas, top two scoops of ice cream with the peach halves, drizzle with raspberry sauce and scatter with a few extra raspberries.

HOT CHOCOLATE FUDGE SUNDAE

The ice cream needs to be very cold and firm for this sundae.

SERVES 4
Rich chocolate sauce to taste
4 large scoops chilli chocolate ice cream
4 large scoops vanilla ice cream
1 tub clotted cream
Grated dark chocolate and white
    chocolate to decorate

Warm the rich chocolate sauce until hot but not boiling.

Place one large scoop of chilli chocolate ice cream in the bottom of each sundae glass, add a large scoop of vanilla ice cream and drizzle to taste with the warm rich chocolate sauce. Top with a spoonful of clotted cream and sprinkle with grated dark and white chocolate.

GREAT SHAKES

Remember to place the ice cream in the fridge until it becomes soft scoop, before mixing your shake,

BLUEBERRY & VANILLA SHAKE

A great base recipe for any soft fruit or ice cream flavour. Blitz and enjoy.

SERVES 2
2 large scoops vanilla ice cream
275ml/½ pint cold full-fat milk
110g/4oz blueberries, plus a few extra
   to serve
Half a teaspoon vanilla extract
Honey to taste

Blitz the ice cream, milk, blueberries and vanilla in a liquidizer until thick and smooth. Sweeten with honey to taste, pour into chilled tall glasses and decorate with a few blueberries.

PINA COLADA SHAKE

A splash of rum anyone?

SERVES 2
2 scoops vanilla ice cream
275ml/½ pint chilled coconut milk
110g/4oz diced fresh pineapple, plus an extra slice to garnish
Half a small banana, peeled and cut into chunks

Whizz all the ingredients in a liquidizer until smooth, pour into glasses and decorate the rim with an extra chunk of pineapple.

MANGO & CARDAMOM SHAKE

The texture and flavour of cheat's no-churn ice cream blends with fresh mango and cardamom to make an Indian lassi-style shake.

SERVES 2
2 large scoops cheat's no-churn ice cream
275ml/½ pint cold whole milk
1 small ripe mango, peeled and cubed
¼ teaspoon ground cardamom, plus extra to serve
Maple syrup to taste

Blitz everything together in a liquidizer until smooth, pour into chilled glasses and sprinkle with extra cardamom to serve.

LUSCIOUS LOLLIES

The beauty of homemade ice lollies is you know exactly what's in them! Kids love to help make these pure fruit lollies that are guaranteed additive-free.

There are various inexpensive lolly moulds available to buy. Alternatively small-sized paper cups with a stick inserted in the middle also do the trick.

All the recipes make six 100ml/3½fl oz lollies.

MIXED BERRY MINI MILKS

250g/9oz frozen mixed berries
200ml/7fl oz natural yoghurt
Honey to taste

Blend the berries and yoghurt in a food processor until smooth. Sweeten with honey to taste, pour into lolly moulds and freeze overnight.

APPLE & POMEGRANATE LOLLY

Mix and match the fruit purée and juice in this recipe to concoct your own original lolly. Ripe strawberries make a sensational alternative!

350g/12oz apple purée (either buy unsweetened 100% apple purée
   or make your own)
200ml/7fl oz pomegranate juice

Whisk all the ingredients together, pour into lolly moulds and freeze overnight.

BANANAS & CREAM LOLLY

2 large ripe bananas, peeled and cut into chunks
250ml/9 fl oz crème fraîche
4 tablespoons unsweetened apple juice
2 tablespoons clear honey
A good pinch of cinnamon

Blend the bananas, crème fraîche, apple juice, honey and cinnamon in a food processor until smooth. Pour into lolly moulds and freeze overnight.

INDEX OF RECIPES